The Simplify-Your-Life Quote Book

OVER 500 INSPIRING QUOTATIONS TO
HELP YOU RELAX, REFOCUS, AND RENEW

Compiled by **Allen Klein**

GRAMERCY BOOKS
NEW YORK

For my friends Kevin and Will,
whose lives are simple yet rich.

This 2005 edition is published by Gramercy Books, an imprint of Random House Value Publishing, a division of Random House, Inc., New York.

Gramercy is a registered trademark and the colophon is a trademark of Random House, Inc.

Random House
New York • Toronto • London • Sydney • Auckland
www.randomhouse.com

Interior book design by Karen Ocker

Printed and bound in Singapore

Library of Congress Cataloging-in-Publication Data
The simplify-your-life quote book over 500 inspiring quotations to help you relax, refocus, and renew / compiled by Allen Klein.
p. cm.
Includes index.
ISBN 0-517-22462-3
I. Conduct of life—Quotations, maxims, etc. I. Klein, Allen.

PN6084.C556S62 2005
080—dc22

2005045978

10 9 8 7 6 5 4 3 2 1

CONTENTS

INTRODUCTION

While writing this book, I was extremely busy. My speaking schedule was full, I was working on several other projects, and I was about to become the president of the Association for Applied and Therapeutic Humor. Here I was compiling information about how to make your life simpler and mine was getting more complicated everyday.

Then I started to take the advice of the quotations I was gathering. What I found was that their words helped me slow down, prioritize what was most important, and actually get more done in a calmer, more relaxed, frame of mind.

It has been said that we teach what we need to learn. Obviously, I needed to hear about the wisdom of simplicity. I learned a lot from this book. I hope you do too.

ALLEN KLEIN,
SAN FRANCISCO

**Our life is frittered away by detail...
simplify, simplify.**

HENRY DAVID THOREAU

Paradise is where I am.

VOLTAIRE

**One of the ultimate objectives of attaining inner simplicity
is to learn to live happily in the present moment.**

ELAINE ST. JAMES

**We do not remember days,
we remember moments.**

CESARE PAVESE

**Life is a succession of moments.
To live each one is to succeed.**

CORITA KENT

**The more I give myself permission to live in the moment
and enjoy it without feeling guilty or judgmental about any
other time, the better I feel about the quality of my work.**

WAYNE DYER

Living in the moment means letting go of the past and
not waiting for the future. It means living your life consciously,
aware that each moment you breathe is a gift.

OPRAH WINFREY

Make it a rule of life never to regret and never to look back.
Regret is an appalling waste of energy; you can't build on it;
it's only good for wallowing in.

KATHERINE MANSFIELD

It is only possible to live happily ever after
on a day to day basis.

MARGARET BONNANO

Reflect upon your present blessings, of which
every man has many—not on your past misfortunes,
of which all men have some.

CHARLES DICKENS

Look to this day!
For it is life, the very life of life.

KALIDASA

To live is so startling,
it leaves little time for anything else.

EMILY DICKINSON

It's not that "today is the first day of the rest of your life,"
but that now is all there is of my life.

HUGH PRATHER

How we spend our days is, of course, how we spend our lives.

ANNIE DILLARD

The ideal day never comes.
Today is ideal for him who makes it so.

HORATIO DRESSER

If we are ever to enjoy life, now is the time. . . .
Today should always be our most wonderful day.

THOMAS DREIER

Only that day dawns to which we are awake.

HENRY DAVID THOREAU

It's only when we truly know and understand that we have a limited time on earth—and that we have no way of knowing when our time is up—that we will begin to live each day to the fullest, as if it was the only one we had.

ELISABETH KÜBLER-ROSS

May you live every day of your life.

JONATHAN SWIFT

There is only one world, the world pressing against you at this minute. There is only one minute in which you are alive, this minute here and now. The only way to live is by accepting each minute as an unrepeatable miracle.

STORM JAMESON

Every day we are engaged in a miracle which we don't even recognize: a blue sky, white clouds, green leaves, the black, curious eyes of a child—our own two eyes. All is a miracle.

THICH NHAT HANH

Today a new sunrise for me; everything lives,
everything is animated, everything seems to speak to me
of my passion, everything invites me to cherish it.

ANNE DE LENCLOS

The moment one gives close attention to anything,
even a blade of grass, it becomes, a mysterious, awesome,
indescribably magnificent world in itself.

HENRY MILLER

Finally it has penetrated my thick skull.
This life—this moment—is no dress rehearsal. This is it!

FLETCHER KNEBEL

"Now thyself" is more important than "Know thyself."
Reason is what tells us to ignore the present and live in the future.
So all we do is make plans. We think that somewhere there are
going to be green pastures. It's crazy. Heaven is nothing
but a grand, monumental instance of future.
Listen, now is good. Now is wonderful.

MEL BROOKS

The experience of eternity right here and now is the function of life.
Heaven is not the place to have the experience,
here's the place to have the experience.

JOSEPH CAMPBELL

These are the good old days.

ANONYMOUS

Do not look back on happiness, or dream of it in the future.
You are only sure of today; do not let yourself be cheated out of it.

HENRY WARD BEECHER

The present moment is significant, not as the bridge between
past and future, but by reason of its contents, which can fill our
emptiness and become ours, if we are capable of receiving them.

DAG HAMMARSKJÖLD

Accept yourself, your physical condition, and your fate
as they are at the present moment.

MORRIE SCHWARTZ

Love the moment and the energy of the moment
will spread beyond all boundaries.

CORITA KENT

Do what you can, with what you have, where you are.

THEODORE ROOSEVELT

When you stop comparing what is right here and now
with what you wish were, you can begin to enjoy what is.

CHERI HUBER

Spend the afternoon.
You can't take it with you.

ANNIE DILLARD

I try to learn from the past, but I plan for the future
by focusing exclusively on the present. That's where the fun is.

DONALD TRUMP

The secret of health for both mind and body is
not to mourn for the past, nor to worry about the future,
but to live the present moment wisely and earnestly.

BUDDHA

The present contains all that there is.
It is holy ground, for it is the past, and it is the future.

ALFRED NORTH WHITEHEAD

The art of life is to live in the present moment, and to make that
moment as perfect as we can by the realization that we are
the instruments and expression of God Himself.

EMMET FOX

If I am incapable of washing dishes joyfully, if I want to finish them
quickly so I can go and have dessert, I will be equally incapable of
enjoying my dessert. With the fork in hand, I will be thinking about
what to do next, and the texture and flavor of the dessert, together
with the pleasure of eating it, will be lost. I will always be dragged
into the future, never able to live in the present moment.

THICH NHAT HANH

You don't own the future, you don't own the past.
Today is all you have.

LES BROWN

You can clutch the past so tightly to your chest that it leaves your arms too full to embrace the present.

JAN GLIDEWELL

The past exists only in our memories, the future only in our plans. The present is our only reality.

ROBERT PIRSIG

It is difficult to live in the present, ridiculous to live in the future, and impossible to live in the past. Nothing is as far away as one minute ago.

JIM BISHOP

I live now and only now, and I will do what I want to do this moment and not what I decided was best for me yesterday.

HUGH PRATHER

Don't make the mistake of letting yesterday use up too much of today.

ANONYMOUS

**Do not boast about tomorrow, for
you do not know what a day may bring forth.**

PROVERBS 27:1

One today is worth two tomorrows.

BENJAMIN FRANKLIN

Leave tomorrow until tomorrow.

GERMAN PROVERB

**The best thing about the future
is that it comes only one day at a time.**

ABRAHAM LINCOLN

Besides the noble art of getting things done,
there is the noble art of leaving things undone.
The wisdom of life consists in the elimination of non-essentials.

LIN YUTANG

The great secret of life [is] not to open your letters for a fortnight.
At the expiration of that period you will find that nearly all of them
have answered themselves.

ARTHUR BINSTEAD

I do not take a single newspaper, nor read one a month,
and I feel myself infinitely the happier for it.

THOMAS JEFFERSON

Don't answer the phone just because it's ringing.

ELAINE ST. JAMES

If someone throws you the ball,
you don't have to catch it.

RICHARD CARLSON

There is one piece of advice, in a life of study,
which I think no one will object to; and that is,
every now and then to be completely idle—do nothing at all.

SYDNEY SMITH

The Master arrives without leaving,
sees the light without looking,
achieves without doing a thing.

LAO-TZU

If it's working, keep doing it.
If it's not working, stop doing it.
If you don't know what to do, don't do anything.

MELVIN KONNER

To do great work, a man must be very idle
as well as very industrious.

SAMUEL BUTLER

He lacks much who has no aptitude for idleness.

LOUISE BEEBE WILDER

He does not seem to me to be a free man
who does not sometimes do nothing.

CICERO

It's not enough to be busy... the question is:
What are we busy about?

HENRY DAVID THOREAU

The Chinese word for "busy" consists of two parts.
One part symbolizes the human heart, the other part
symbolizes death. The meaning that can be extrapolated
is that when one is excessively busy, his heart is dead.

CHIN-NING CHU

I have a very full and busy life and occasionally am asked, "Scotty,
how can you do all that you do?" There are multiple answers... but
the most telling reply I can give is: "Because I spend at least two
hours a day doing nothing." Ironically, the questioner usually
responds by saying he's too busy to do that.

M. SCOTT PECK

To do nothing is in every man's power.

SAMUEL JOHNSON

Each week, watch one fewer hour-long television show.

JEFF DAVIDSON

You have to allow a certain amount of time in which you are doing nothing in order to have things occur to you, to let your mind think.

MORTIMER ADLER

To do nothing is sometimes a good remedy.

HIPPOCRATES

**Guard the senses and life is ever full...
always be busy and life is beyond hope.**

LAO-TZU

If you can spend a perfectly useless afternoon in a perfectly useless manner, you have learned how to live.

LIN YUTANG

Leave all the afternoon for exercise and recreation, which are as necessary as reading. I will rather say more necessary because health is worth more than learning.

THOMAS JEFFERSON

Never again clutter your days or nights with so many menial
and unimportant things that you have no time to accept a real
challenge when it comes along. . . . No more busy work. . . .
Leave time, leave space, to grow.

OG MANDINO

Leisure and the cultivation of human capacities
are inextricably interdependent.

MARGARET MEAD

A broad margin of leisure is as beautiful in a man's life
as in a book. Haste makes waste, no less in life than
in housekeeping. Keep the time, observe the hours
of the universe, not of the cars.

HENRY DAVID THOREAU

Take time to come home to yourself everyday.

ROBIN CASARJEAN

Guard well your spare moments. They are like uncut diamonds.

RALPH WALDO EMERSON

I would not exchange my leisure hours
for all the wealth in the world.

COMTE DE MIRABEAU

It's not easy saying no. We're so used to thinking we should
be able to taste every darned thing on the banquet table
that we wind up not enjoying any of it.

JANET LUHRS

No one can maintain more than three priorities. . . .
Figure out what your priorities are, and say no to everything else.

ELAINE ST. JAMES

Tell him to live by yes and no—
yes to everything good, no to everything bad.

WILLIAM JAMES

There is no pleasure in having nothing to do;
the fun is in having lots to do—and not doing it.

MARY WILSON LITTLE

I've learned that you can't have everything
and do everything at the same time.

OPRAH WINFREY

To do two things at once is to do neither.

PUBLILIUS SYRUS

**Trying to remember too many things is certainly one of
the major sources of psychologic stress. I make a conscious
effort to forget immediately all that is unimportant
and to jot down data of possible value.**

HANS SELYE

Always do one thing less than you think you can do.

BERNARD BARUCH

Less is more.

MIES VAN DER ROHE

Focus on

What's
Important

Often people attempt to live their lives backwards:
they try to have more things, or more money, in order to
do more of what they want so that they will be happier.
The way it actually works is the reverse. You must first
be who you really are, then, do what you need to do,
in order to have what you want.

MARGARET YOUNG

What really matters is what you do with what you have.

SHIRLEY LORD

You have to accept whatever comes and the only important thing is
that you meet it with the best you have to give.

ELEANOR ROOSEVELT

The great opportunity is where you are. Do not despise
your own place and hour. Every place is under the stars,
every place is the center of the world.

JOHN BURROUGHS

I always say to myself, what is the most important thing
we can think about at this extraordinary moment.

FRANCOIS DUC DE LA ROCHEFOUCAULD

The best things in life are nearest: Breath in your nostrils,
light in your eyes, flowers at your feet, duties at your hand,
the path of right just before you.

ROBERT LOUIS STEVENSON

You're only here for a short visit. Don't hurry, don't worry.
And be sure to smell the flowers along the way.

WALTER HAGEN

In the hope of reaching the moon, men fail to see the flowers
that blossom at their feet.

ALBERT SCHWEITZER

Millions of persons long for immortality who do not know
what to do with themselves on a rainy afternoon.

SUSAN ERTZ

To find the universal elements enough; to find the air and the
water exhilarating, to be refreshed by a morning walk
or an evening saunter... to be thrilled by the stars at night;
to be elated over a bird's nest or a wildflower in spring
—these are some of the rewards of the simple life.

JOHN BURROUGHS

If you wish to know the divine,
feel the wind on your face and the warm sun on your hand.

BUDDHA

Get pleasure out of life... as much as you can.
Nobody ever died from pleasure.

SOL HUROK

If you break your neck, if you have nothing to eat,
if your house is on fire—then you got a problem.
Everything else is inconvenience.

ROBERT FULGHUM

One way to get high blood pressure
is to go mountain climbing over molehills.

EARL WILSON

Get your priorities straight. Looking back, no one ever wished that he or she had returned more phone calls or attended more meetings.

ODETTE POLLAR

Why not spend some time in determining what is worthwhile for us, and then go after that?

WILLIAM ROSS

If I die tomorrow,
I hope I've spent this day doing what I truly want to do and not picking up the dry cleaning and going to the salmon sale at Safeway.

LYNN BEFERA

I have only one life and it is short enough.
Why waste it on things I don't want most?

LOUIS BRANDEIS

You decide what it is you want to accomplish and then you lay out your plans to get there, and then you just do it. It's pretty straightforward.

NANCY DITZ

Live your life each day as you would climb a mountain.
An occasional glance towards the summit keeps the goal in mind,
but many beautiful scenes are to be observed
from each new vantage point.

HAROLD B. MELCHART

What is the center of your life? Carefully examine where you spend
your attention, your time. Look at your appointment book, your
daily schedule. . . . This is what receives your care and attention—
and by definition, your love.

WAYNE MULLER

I was rich, if not in money, in sunny hours and summer days,
and spent them lavishly.

HENRY DAVID THOREAU

I don't think God puts you on this earth just to make millions of
dollars and ignore everything else.

CHRIS AMUNDSEN

**Keep your job and your life in perspective.
Success at the expense of relaxation and enjoyment is no success.**

ODETTE POLLAR

**It's not the honors and the prizes and the fancy outsides of life
that ultimately nourish our souls. It's the knowing
that we can be trusted, that we never have to fear the truth,
that the bedrock of our very being is firm.**

FRED ROGERS

**Know what's important to you. Ask yourself what really matters
in your relationships, your work, and for you individually.
Then ask yourself: "Do I spend my time on things that really matter
to me? Or do I spend time on other people's goals?"**

DANIEL AMEN

Don't let other people tell you what you want.

PAT RILEY

**Time is the coin of your life. It is the only coin you have,
and only you can determine how it will be spent.
Be careful lest you let other people spend it for you.**

CARL SANDBURG

I am thankful for small mercies. I compared notes with one
of my friends who expects everything of the universe, and is
disappointed when anything is less than the best, and I found
that I begin at the other extreme, expecting nothing,
and am always full of thanks for moderate goods.

RALPH WALDO EMERSON

Enjoy the little things, for one day you may look back
and realize they were the big things.

ROBERT BRAULT

The little things? The little moments? They aren't little.

JON KABAT-ZINN

Don't be afraid to give your best to what seemingly are small jobs.
Every time you conquer one it makes you that much stronger.
If you do the little jobs well, the big ones will tend
to take care of themselves.

DALE CARNEGIE

Despise not small things. . . .
A spark is a little thing, yet it may kindle the world.

MARTIN FARQUHAR TUPPER

The gifts we treasure most over the years are often small and simple.
In easy times and in tough times, what seems to matter most
is the way we show those nearest us that we've been listening
to their needs, to their joys, and to their challenges.

FRED ROGERS

All the wonderful things in life are so simple that one is
not aware of their wonder until they are beyond touch.

FRANCES GUNTHER

The simple life is one in which there is always time to remember
the divine purpose behind each of our tasks, time to listen for a
possible divine amendment to the day's schedule, and time to be
thankful for the divine presence at each moment of the day.

LLOYD LEE WILSON

The ordinary arts we practice everyday at home are of
more importance to the soul than their simplicity might suggest.

THOMAS MOORE

A morning-glory at my window satisfies me more
than the metaphysics of books.

WALT WHITMAN

It isn't the great big pleasures that count the most,
it's making a great deal out of the little ones.

JEAN WEBSTER

To poke a wood fire is more solid enjoyment
than almost anything else in the world.

CHARLES DUDLEY WARNER

If people concentrated on the really important things in life,
there'd be a shortage of fishing poles.

DOUG LARSON

The next time you buy a microwaveable "dinner for two,"
think about the hour of free time you just gained.
Then spend that hour on something really important to you.

ODETTE POLLAR

It is not what we take up, but what we give up, that makes us rich.

HENRY WARD BEECHER

The art of being wise is the art of knowing what to overlook.

WILLIAM JAMES

The most important thing is to have a code of life,
to know how to live.

HANS SELYE

We all have 100% to deal with in our lives: 10% is important,
90% unimportant. The secret to a happy, productive life
is to deal with the 10% and let the 90% slip.

SALLI RASBERRY AND PADI SELWYN

Throw away your televisions. Practice critical thinking.
Communicate with your family. Have social intercourse
with your children. Play with them. Sing with them
around the piano. Dance with them. Be foolish with them.
Go out into the garden and have time to yourself.

HELEN CALDICOTT

What lies behind us and what lies before us
are tiny matters compared to what lies within us.

OLIVER WENDELL HOLMES

Remember, what you possess in the world will be found
at the day of your death to belong to someone else,
but what you are will be yours forever.

HENRY VAN DYKE

Though we travel the world over to find the beautiful,
we must carry it with us or we find it not.

RALPH WALDO EMERSON

I like living. I have sometimes been wildly, despairingly, acutely
miserable, racked with sorrow, but through it all I still know quite
certainly that just to be alive is a grand thing.

AGATHA CHRISTIE

How easily we get trapped in that which is not essential—in looking
good, winning at competition, gathering power and wealth—when
simply being alive is the gift beyond measure.

PARKER J. PALMER

"I can forgive, but I can not forget" is another way of saying,
"I will not forgive."

HENRY WARD BEECHER

Life is an exercise in forgiveness.

NORMAN COUSINS

To err is human, to forgive, divine.

ALEXANDER POPE

Learn to forgive yourself and to forgive others.
Ask for forgiveness from others. Forgiveness can soften the heart,
drain the bitterness, and dissolve your guilt.

MORRIE SCHWARTZ

He who cannot forgive others destroys the bridge
over which he himself must pass.

GEORGE HERBERT

Forgive and you will be forgiven.

LUKE 6:37

The creativity and positive energy you put forth come back
to you many times over. So do the hurt and destruction.
Which would you rather get back?

RALPH MARSTON

To forgive is the highest, most beautiful form of love.
In return, you will receive untold peace and happiness.

ROBERT MULLER

Those who are at war with others
are not at peace with themselves.

WILLIAM HAZLITT

Knowing life is short,
How can we quarrel?

BUDDHA

If you want to get along, go along.

SAM RAYBURN

To be wronged is nothing unless
you continue to remember it.

CONFUCIUS

If there's one pitch you keep swinging at and keep missing,
stop swinging at it.

YOGI BERRA

Leave old baggage behind;
the less you carry, the farther you go.

ANONYMOUS

May I forget what ought to be forgotten; and recall, unfailing,
all that ought to be recalled, each kindly thing,
forgetting what might sting.

MARY CAROLYN DAVIES

Keeping score of old scores and scars, getting even
and one-upping, always make you less than you are.

MALCOLM FORBES

You never get ahead of anyone
as long as you try to get even with him.

LOU HOLTZ

**Reject your sense of injury
and the injury itself disappears.**

MARCUS AURELIUS

**I can have peace of mind
only when I forgive rather than judge.**

GERALD JAMPOLSKY

**Always forgive your enemies;
nothing annoys them so much.**

OSCAR WILDE

**Resentment is like taking poison
and waiting for the other person to die.**

MALACHY MCCOURT

**Forgiveness is a funny thing.
It warms the heart and cools the sting.**

WILLIAM A. WARD

**Forgiveness is the answer to the child's dream of a miracle
by which what is broken is made whole again,
what is soiled is again made clean.**

CATHERINE PONDER

In the end, forgiveness simply means
never putting another person out of our heart.

JACK KORNFIELD

Forgiveness is the key to action and freedom.

HANNAH ARENDT

If you want to see the brave, look for those who can forgive.

BHAGAVAD-GITA

The weak can never forgive.
Forgiveness is the attribute of the strong.

MAHATMA GANDHI

I believe with all my heart that civilization has produced nothing
finer than a man or woman who thinks and practices true tolerance.

FRANK KNOX

Forgiveness means letting go of the past.

GERALD JAMPOLSKY

When you forgive, you in no way change the past—
but you sure do change the future.

BERNARD MELTZER

Never do anything when you are in a temper, ✓
for you will do everything wrong.

BALTASAR GRACIÁN

The elephant is never won with anger.

EARL OF ROCHESTER

Anyone can become angry—that is easy. But to be angry with the
right person, to the right degree, at the right time, for the right pur-
pose, and in the right way—that is not easy.

ARISTOTLE

The more anger towards the past you carry in your heart, ✓
the less capable you are of loving in the present.

BARBARA DE ANGELIS

For every minute you are angry, ✓
you lose sixty seconds of happiness.

RALPH WALDO EMERSON

Anger is a lot like a piece of shredded wheat caught
under your dentures. If you leave it there you'll
get a blister and you gotta eat Jell-o all week.
If you get rid of it, the sore heals and you feel better.

SOPHIA PETRILLO, "THE GOLDEN GIRLS"

Write injuries in dust, benefits in marble.

BENJAMIN FRANKLIN

Ask yourself this question:
"Will this matter a year from now?"

RICHARD CARLSON

Better bend than break.

H. G. BOHN

**The bamboo that bends is stronger
than the oak that resists.**

JAPANESE PROVERB

If you can't fight and you can't flee, flow.

ROBERT S. ELIOT

It's much easier to ride the horse in the direction he's going.

WERNER ERHARD

You have freedom when you're easy in your harness.

ROBERT FROST

**Develop a mind that is vast like the water, where experiences
both pleasant and unpleasant can appear and disappear without
conflict, struggle, or harm. Rest in a mind like vast water.**

BUDDHA

**I began to have an idea of my life, not as the slow shaping of
achievement to fit my preconceived purposes, but as the gradual
discovery and growth of a purpose which I did not know.**

JOANNA FIELD

Sometimes you've got to let everything go—purge yourself.
If you are unhappy with anything... whatever is bringing you down,
get rid of it. Because you'll find that when you're free,
your true creativity, your true self comes out.

TINA TURNER

Somehow, when we no longer feel in control,
we become available to deeper aliveness.

RICHARD MOSS

Not trying to go faster or slower,
be still, and let go.
Just let things be
for it is exactly as it should be.

SOSAN

Things turn out best for the people who make the best
of the way things turn out.

JOHN WOODEN

Live with less grasping and
more appreciation and caring.

JACK KORNFIELD

Eventually I lost interest in trying to control my life,
to make things happen in a way that I thought I wanted them to be.
I began to practice surrendering to the universe and
finding out what "it" wanted me to do.

SHAKTI GAWAIN

As your faith is strengthened, you will find that there is
no longer the need to have a sense of control, that things
will flow as they will, and that you will flow with them,
to your great delight and benefit.

EMMANUEL TENEY

There is no good in arguing with the inevitable. The only argument
available with an east wind is to put on your overcoat.

JAMES RUSSELL LOWELL

When you're in a state of nonacceptance, it's difficult to learn.
A clenched fist cannot receive a gift, and a clenched psyche—
grasped tightly against the reality of what must not be accepted—
cannot easily receive a lesson.

JOHN-ROGER AND PETER MCWILLIAMS

You can't fit a square peg into a round hole. . . .
Think how simple your life would be if you eliminated the difficult
things—the things that probably weren't meant to be anyway—and
concentrated on doing what was easy.

ELAINE ST. JAMES

The worst thing you can do is to try to cling to something
that's gone, or to recreate it.

JOHNETTE NAPOLITANO

The bird of paradise alights
only upon the hand that does not grasp.

JOHN BERRY

Return to the beginning;
Become a child again.

LAO-TZU

Genius is the ability to regain childhood at will.

ANONYMOUS

Youth would be an ideal state if it came a little later in life.

HERBERT HENRY ASQUITH

You can learn new things at any time in your life
if you're willing to be a beginner. If you actually learn to
like being a beginner, the whole world opens up to you.

BARBARA SHER

The parents exist to teach the child,
but also they must learn what the child has to teach them,
and the child has a very great deal to teach them.

ARNOLD BENNETT

The first problem for all of us, men and women,
is not to learn, but to unlearn.

GLORIA STEINEM

My music is best understood by children and animals.

IGOR STRAVINSKY

There are children playing in the streets who could solve some of my top problems in physics, because they have modes of sensory perception that I lost long ago.

J. ROBERT OPPENHEIMER

Wisdom sends us back to our childhood.

BLAISE PASCAL

**Seek the wisdom of the ages,
but look at the world through the eyes of a child.**

RON WILD

**Look at everything as though you were seeing it
either for the first or last time.**

BETTY SMITH

The voyage of discovery lies not in finding new landscapes,
but in having new eyes.

MARCEL PROUST

As great scientists have said and as all children know,
it is above all by the imagination that we achieve perception,
and compassion, and hope.

URSULA LEGUIN

It is the childlike mind that finds the kingdom.

CHARLES FILLMORE

If help and salvation are to come, they can only come from
the children, for the children are the makers of men.

MARIA MONTESSORI

If my heart can become pure and simple like that of a child,
I think there probably can be no greater happiness than this.

KITARO NISHIDA

Is nothing in life ever straight and clear, the way children see it?

ROSIE THOMAS

Pretty much all the honest truth telling there is in the world
is done by children.

OLIVER WENDELL HOLMES

In every real man a child is hidden that wants to play.

FRIEDRICH WILHELM NIETZSCHE

It is paradoxical that many educators and parents still differentiate
between a time for learning and a time for play
without seeing the vital connection between them.

LEO BUSCAGLIA

In reality, we are still children. We want to find a playmate
for our thoughts and feelings.

WILHELM STEKEL

Man is most nearly himself when he achieves the seriousness
of a child at play.

HERACLITUS

We live in an ironic society where even play is turned into work,
but the highest existence is not work;
the highest level of existence is play.

CONRAD HYERS

People do not quit playing because they grow old.
They grow old because they quit playing.

OLIVER WENDELL HOLMES

Can you imagine experiencing the world as a great sandbox
given for us to play in like we did as children? As we play,
we can also open ourselves to the exploration of our edges,
always creating new adventures of self-exploration as we
let go of old out-dated beliefs about ourselves.

JUDITH-ANNETTE MILBURN

It may well be that all games are silly.
But then—so are human beings.

ROBERT LYND

**If it seems a childish thing to do,
do it in remembrance that you were a child.**

FREDERICK BUECHNER

Hang around doggies and kids: they know how to play.

GEOFFREY GODBEY

The child is in me still... and sometimes not so still.

FRED ROGERS

**If you listen carefully to children
you will have plenty about which to laugh.**

STEVE ALLEN

**Know you what it is to be a child? It is to be something very
different from the man of today. It is to have a spirit yet steaming
from the water of baptism; it is to believe in love, to believe in
loveliness, to believe in belief; it is to be so little that the elves can
reach to whisper in your ear; it is to turn pumpkins into coaches,
and mice into horses, lowness into loftiness, and nothing into
everything, for each child has its fairy godmother in its soul.**

FRANCIS THOMPSON

**Every child comes with the message
that God is not yet tired of the man.**

RABINDRANATH TAGORE

**The secret of genius is
to carry the spirit of the child into old age.**

THOMAS HUXLEY

**Great is the man who has
not lost his childlike heart.**

MENCIUS

**By learning to act more like a child, human beings can revolution-
ize their lives and become for the first time, perhaps, the kinds of
creatures their heritage has prepared them to be—
youthful all the days of their lives.**

ASHLEY MONTAGU

Have Less

The most important things in life aren't things.

ANONYMOUS

If there is to be any peace it will come through being, not having.

HENRY MILLER

**Most of the luxuries, and many of the so-called comforts of life,
are not only not indispensable, but positive hindrances
to the elevation of mankind.**

HENRY DAVID THOREAU

Joy is not in things; it is in us.

RICHARD WAGNER

Be not anxious about what you have, but about what you are.

POPE ST. GREGORY I

**Superfluous wealth can buy superfluities only.
Money is not required to buy one necessity of the soul.**

HENRY DAVID THOREAU

True abundance is not about gathering more things,
it's about touching the place in us that is connected to the
divine source of abundance, so that we know what we
need in the moment will be provided.

MARY MANIN MORRISSEY

Own only what you can always carry with you; know languages,
know countries, know people. Let your memory be your travel bag.

ALEXANDER SOLZHENITSYN

Be content with what you have, rejoice in the way things are.
When you realize there is nothing lacking,
the whole world belongs to you.

LAO-TZU

Use it up, wear it out, make it do, or do without.

NEW ENGLAND PROVERB

We never buy more than we need.
We never need more than we use.
We never use more than
It takes to get by
Til we learn to need less.

CHINESE PROVERB

Have fewer things and see each of them better.

ODETTE POLLAR

**Know what is enough. If you think that having more
is what is going to produce happiness
or contentment or any positive attribute,
will you ever get there?**

JOE DOMINGUEZ

**You have succeeded in life when all you really want
is only what you really need.**

VERNON HOWARD

**Make peace with the awareness that you can't have everything you
want. It's more important for you to get everything you need.
Contentment comes when our essential needs are met.**

SARAH BAN BREATHNACH

If you always want "more" you will never have "enough."

KEN KEYES, JR. AND BRUCE BURKAN

There must be more to life than having everything.

MAURICE SENDAK

You can't have it all—where would you put it?

STEVEN WRIGHT

You can have anything you want.
You just can't have everything you want.

JOHN-ROGER AND PETER McWILLIAMS

You can never get enough of what you don't need
to make you happy.

ERIC HOFFER

If men could regard the events of their own lives
with more open minds, they would frequently discover
that they did not really desire the things
they failed to obtain.

EMILE HERZOG

Some luck lies in not getting what you thought you wanted,
but getting what you have, which once you have got it
you may be smart enough to see is what you
would have wanted had you known.

GARRISON KEILLOR

My riches consist not in the extent of my possessions,
but in the fewness of my wants.

J. BROTHERTON

We don't need to increase our goods nearly as much
as we need to scale down our wants.
Not wanting something is as good as possessing it.

DONALD HORBAN

When you can't have what you want,
it's time to start wanting what you have.

KATHLEEN A. SUTTON

He who is attached to things will suffer much.

LAO-TZU

Possessions are usually diminished by possession.

FRIEDRICH WILHELM NIETZSCHE

**Simplicity is not so much about what we own,
but about what owns us.**

CHRISTIN HADLEY SNYDER

All things that a man owns hold him far more than he holds them.

SIGRID UNDSET

**It is preoccupation with possessions, more than anything else,
that prevents us from living freely and nobly.**

BERTRAND RUSSELL

He who buys what he does not need steals from himself.

ANONYMOUS

**Possession of material riches without inner peace
is like dying of thirst while bathing in the river.**

PARAMAHANSA YOGANANDA

Those who want the fewest things
are nearest to the gods.

SOCRATES

Happiness resides not in possessions and not in gold,
the feeling of happiness dwells in the soul.

DEMOCRITUS

As for things, how they do accumulate,
how often I wish to exclaim,
"Oh don't give me that!"

SUSAN HALE

The more we reduce the size of our world,
the more we shall be its master.

JACINTO BENAVENTE

Through the years I have found it wonderful to acquire,
but it is also wonderful to divest. It's rather like exhaling.

HELEN HAYES

Reduce the complexity of life by eliminating the needless
wants of life, and the labors of life reduce themselves.

EDWIN WAY TEALE

That man is the richest whose
pleasures are the cheapest.

HENRY DAVID THOREAU

Frugality is one of the most beautiful and joyful words
in the English language, and yet one that we are culturally
cut off from understanding and enjoying. The consumption society
has made us feel that happiness lies in having things, and has
failed to teach us the happiness of not having things.

ELISE BOULDING

One day I had the sudden realization: If I stopped buying things
right this moment, there is no way I could ever use all I have now.

DON ASLETT

To know you have enough is to be rich.

LAO-TZU

The richest person is the one who is contented with what he has.

ROBERT C. SAVAGE

Even though you have ten thousand fields,
you can eat no more than one measure of rice a day.
Even though your dwelling contains a hundred rooms,
you can use but eight feet of space a night.

CHINESE PROVERB

Riches do not consist in the possession of treasures,
but in the use made of them.

NAPOLEON BONAPARTE

If you want a golden rule that will fit everybody, this is it:
Have nothing in your house that you do not know
to be useful or believe to be beautiful.

WILLIAM MORRIS

Too many people spend money they haven't earned, to buy things
they don't want, to impress people they don't like.

WILL ROGERS

Normal is getting dressed in clothes that you buy for work, driving
through traffic in a car that you are still paying for, in order to
get to the job that you need so you can pay for the clothes,
car, and the house that you leave empty all day
in order to afford to live in it.

ELLEN GOODMAN

Let the potent power of simplicity begin to work in your life.
When in doubt, live without.

SARAH BAN BREATHNACH

Notice to Guests: If there is anything you need and don't see,
please let us know, we will show you how to do without it.

MARY McWILLIAMS FADDEN

To be without some of the things you want
is an indispensable part of happiness.

BERTRAND RUSSELL

Simplicity, simplicity, simplicity! I say let your affairs be as one, two, three and not a hundred or a thousand. . . . We are happy in proportion to the things we can do without.

HENRY DAVID THOREAU

Let your boat of life be light, packed with only what you need.

JEROME K. JEROME

Keep It Simple

'Tis a gift to be simple,
'Tis a gift to be free,

SHAKER HYMN

I have come to understand that making life simpler does
for our minds what getting in shape does for our bodies.

ROBERT LAWRENCE SMITH

In order to seek one's own direction,
one must simplify the mechanics of ordinary everyday life.

PLATO

You know it's time to simplify your life when
you've got a ringing phone in one hand,
a hot double cappuccino mocha in the other,
and you need to make a left-hand turn.

ELAINE ST. JAMES

Achieving simplicity in your life starts with the simple notion
that you are in control. You steer the rudder, flip the switch,
pull the lever, call the shots, and have the power within you
to take steps to make your life simpler.

JEFF DAVIDSON

Voluntary simplicity means going fewer places in one day
rather than more, seeing less so I can see more, doing less
so I can do more, acquiring less so I can have more.

JON KABAT-ZINN

You can't force simplicity; but you can invite it in by
finding as much richness as possible in the few things at hand.
Simplicity doesn't mean meagerness but rather a certain kind
of richness, the fullness that appears when we stop
stuffing the world with things.

THOMAS MOORE

If I were asked to define Quaker simplicity in a nutshell,
I would say that it has little to do with how many things you own
and everything to do with not letting your possessions own you.

ROBERT LAWRENCE SMITH

I am beginning to learn that it is the sweet,
simple things of life which are the real ones after all.

LAURA INGALLS WILDER

The ability to simplify means to eliminate the unnecessary
so that the necessary may speak.

HANS HOFMANN

Simplicity involves unburdening your life, and living more lightly
with fewer distractions that interfere with a high quality life, as
defined uniquely by each individual. You will find people living
simply in large cities, rural areas and everything in between.

LINDA BREEN PIERCE

Life comes together when we seek of the sublime in the ordinary.
Today make discovering those joyful simplicities that bring
you personal comfort and a sense of wellbeing
one of your highest priorities.

SARAH BAN BREATHNACH

It is the simple things of life that make living worthwhile, the sweet
fundamental things such as love and duty, work and rest, and living
close to nature. There are not hothouse blossoms that can compare
in beauty and fragrance with my bouquet of wildflowers.

LAURA INGALLS WILDER

In the end, what affects your life most deeply
are things too simple to talk about.

NELL BLAINE

To live content with small means... this is my symphony.

WILLIAM HENRY CHANNING

To own a bit of ground, to scratch it with a hoe, to plant seeds and watch their renewal of life—this is the commonest delight of the race, the most satisfactory thing a man can do.

CHARLES DUDLEY WARNER

When hungry, eat your rice; when tired, close your eyes. Fools may laugh at me, but wise men will know what I mean.

LIN-CHI

It is difficult to think anything but pleasant thoughts while eating a home-grown tomato.

LEWIS GRIZZARD

You know it's time to simplify your life when you just published your third book on how to get organized, and you can't find it.

ELAINE ST. JAMES

Simplicity doesn't mean to live in misery and poverty.
You have what you need, and you don't want to have
what you don't need.

CHARAN SINGH

Simplicity is the most difficult thing to secure in this
world; it is the last limit of experience
and the last effort of genius.

GEORGE SAND

Simplicity is the nature of great souls.

PAPA RAMADAS

Make everything as simple as possible, but not simpler.

ALBERT EINSTEIN

Any intelligent fool can make things bigger, more complex, and
more violent. It takes a touch of genius—and a lot of courage—
to move in the opposite direction.

E.F. SCHUMACHER

A man must be able to cut a knot, for everything cannot be untied;
he must know how to disengage what is essential from the detail in
which it is enwrapped, for everything cannot be equally considered;
in a word, he must be able to simplify his duties,
his business and his life.

HENRI FREDERIC AMIEL

True simplicity is not the rejection of beauty
in our surroundings, but the refusal to allow concern
for things to clutter our minds.

EDGAR B. CASTLE

Out of clutter, find simplicity.

ALBERT EINSTEIN

Simplicity is the whole secret of well-being.

PETER MATTHIESSEN

In walking, just walk. In sitting, just sit.
Above all, don't wobble.

YUNMEN

**A little simplification would be the first step
toward rational living, I think.**

ELEANOR ROOSEVELT

**I have a simple philosophy. Fill what's empty.
Empty what's full. Scratch where it itches.**

ALICE ROOSEVELT LONGWORTH

**I believe that a simple and unassuming manner of life
is best for everyone, best both for the body and the mind.**

ALBERT EINSTEIN

**Simplicity, clarity, singleness: these are the attributes
that give our lives power and vividness and joy. . . .**

RICHARD HOLLOWAY

Simplicity is the essence of happiness.

CEDRIC BLEDSOE

Purity and simplicity are the two wings with which man soars
above the earth and all temporary nature.

THOMAS Á KEMPIS

In character, in manners, in style, in all things,
the supreme excellence is simplicity.

HENRY WADSWORTH LONGFELLOW

I have learned by some experience, by many examples,
and by the writings of countless others before me,
also occupied in the search, that certain environments,
certain modes of life, certain rules of conduct are more
conducive to inner and outer harmony than others.
There are, in fact, certain roads that one may follow.
Simplification of life is one of them.

ANN MORROW LINDBERGH

Life is really simple,
but we insist on making it complicated.

CONFUCIUS

Life is not complex. We are complex. Life is simple,
and the simple thing is the right thing.

OSCAR WILDE

Manifest plainness,
Embrace simplicity,
Reduce selfishness,
Have few desires.

LAO-TZU

The right thing to do never requires any subterfuge,
it is always simple and direct.

CALVIN COOLIDGE

I searched through rebellion, drugs, diets, mysticism, religions,
intellectualism and much more, only to begin to find... that truth is
basically simple—and feels good, clean and right.

CHICK COREA

All the great things are simple, and many can be expressed in a
single word: freedom; justice; honor; duty; mercy; hope.

SIR WINSTON CHURCHILL

Simplicity of life, even the barest, is not a misery,
but the very foundation of refinement.

WILLIAM MORRIS

Simplicity is the ultimate sophistication.

LEONARDO DA VINCI

In cooking, as in all the arts, simplicity is the sign of perfection.

CURNONSKY

There is no greatness where there is not simplicity.

LEO TOLSTOY

The aspects of things that are most important to us
are hidden because of their simplicity and familiarity.

LUDWIG WITTGENSTEIN

I thank you, my God, for having in a thousand different ways led my
eyes to discover the immense simplicity of things.

PIERRE TEILHARD DE CHARDIN

Rose is a rose is a rose is a rose.

GERTRUDE STEIN

You see, God always takes the simplest way.

ALBERT EINSTEIN

Life is beautiful in its simplicity.

THOMAS MATTHIESSEN

Live simply so others may simply live.

SLOGAN

Speech is silver; silence is golden.

SWISS PROVERB

True silence is the rest of the mind, and is to the spirit what sleep is to the body, nourishment and refreshment.

WILLIAM PENN

In... silence we find a new energy and a real unity. God's energy becomes ours, allowing us to perform things well.

MOTHER TERESA

The first virtue is to restrain the tongue;
he approaches nearest to the gods who knows how to be silent. . . .

CATO THE YOUNGER

Silence is the true friend that never betrays.

CONFUCIUS

The Great Way is empty—
like a vast sky.
Silence the busy mind
and know this perfection.

SOSAN

The deepest feeling always shows itself in silence.

MARIANNE MOORE

**Occasionally in life there are those moments of unutterable
fulfillment which cannot be completely explained by those symbols
called words. Their meanings can only be articulated
by the inaudible language of the heart.**

MARTIN LUTHER KING, JR.

**A loving silence often has far more power to heal and
to connect than the most well-intentioned words.**

RACHEL NAOMI REMEN

**There is something greater and purer than what the mouth utters.
Silence illuminates our souls, whispers to our hearts,
and brings them together.**

KAHLIL GIBRAN

**In the attitude of silence the soul finds the path
in a clearer light, and what is elusive and deceptive
resolves itself into crystal clearness.**

MAHATMA GANDHI

God is the friend of silence. See how nature—trees, flowers, grass—grows in silence; see the stars, the moon and the sun, how they move in silence... we need silence to be able to touch souls.

MOTHER TERESA

Sitting quietly, doing nothing, spring comes, and the grass grows by itself.

ZEN SAYING

We in the "developed" world seem to have many auditory strategies that insulate us from the presence of silence, simplicity, and solitude. When I return to Western culture after time in desert, mountain or forest, I discover how we have filled our world with a multiplicity of noises, a symphony of forgetfulness that keeps our own thoughts and realizations, feelings and intuitions out of audible range.

JOAN HALIFAX

Soon silence will have passed into legend. Man has turned his back on silence. Day after day he invents machines and devices that increase noise and distract humanity from the essence of life, contemplation, meditation.

ANONYMOUS

Why are we embarrassed by silence?
What comfort do we find in all the noise?

MITCH ALBOM

An inability to stay quiet...
is one of the most conspicuous failings of mankind.

WALTER BAGEHOT

The more we elaborate our means of communication,
the less we communicate.

J. B. PRIESTLY

Perhaps it would be a good idea, fantastic as it sounds, to muffle
every telephone, stop every motor and halt all activity for an hour
some day to give people a chance to ponder for a few minutes on
what it is all about, why they are living and what they really want.

JAMES TRUSLOW ADAMS

No one has a finer command of language
than the person who keeps his mouth shut.

SAM RAYBURN

A man is known by the silence he keeps.

OLIVER HERFORD

In Maine we have a saying that there's no point in speaking
unless you can improve on silence.

EDMUND MUSKIE

It's amazing how much you hear
when no one is saying anything.

ELAINE ST. JAMES

There are very few people who don't become more interesting
when they stop talking.

MARY LOWRY

I have never been hurt by anything I didn't say.

CALVIN COOLIDGE

You don't always have to have something to say.

SAMMY DAVIS, JR.

When you have nothing to say, say nothing.

CHARLES CALEB COLTON

**The value of the average conversation
could be enormously improved by the constant use
of four simple words: "I do not know."**

ANDRÉ MAUROIS

**It has been said: lots of things are opened by mistake,
but none so often as the mouth.**

GLADYS CASE

Stop talking and listen to what you really know.

ROBERT LAWRENCE SMITH

**Only in the oasis of silence can we drink deeply
from the inner cup of wisdom.**

SUE PATTON THOELE

A spiritual retreat is medicine for soul starvation. Through silence, solitary practice, and simple living, we begin to fill the empty reservoir. This lifts the veils, dissolves the masks, and creates space within for the feelings of forgiveness, compassion, and loving kindness that are so often blocked.

DAVID A. COOPER

Silence fertilizes the deep place where personality grows. A life with a peaceful center can weather all storms.

NORMAN VINCENT PEALE

One's action ought to come out of an achieved stillness; not to be a mere rushing on.

D. H. LAWRENCE

Well-timed silence is the most commanding expression.

MARK HELPRIN

The silence is as important as the noise. What gets left out is as important as what gets included.

SARA LAWRENCE-LIGHTFOOT

A note of music gains significance
from the silence on either side.

ANNE MORROW LINDBERGH

The notes I handle no better than many pianists. But the pauses
between the notes—ah, that is where the art resides!

ARTUR SCHNABEL

Only in quiet waters do things mirror themselves undistorted.
Only in a quiet mind is adequate perception of the world.

HANS MARGOLIUS

Men cannot see their reflection in running water,
but only in still water.

CHUANG TZU

I have often thought it would be a blessing if each human being
were stricken blind and deaf for a few days during his early adult
life. Darkness would make him more appreciative of sight;
silence would teach him the joys of sound.

HELEN KELLER

To experience reality,
stop using words;
for the more you talk about things,
the farther away from the truth you stray.

SOSAN

Learn to get in touch with silence within yourself and know
that everything in this life has a purpose. There are no mistakes,
no coincidences; all events are blessings given to us to learn from.
There is no need to go to India or anywhere else to find peace.
You will find that deep place of silence right in your room,
your garden, or even your bathtub.

ELISABETH KÜBLER-ROSS

Our language has wisely sensed the two sides of being alone. It has created the word "loneliness" to express the pain of being alone. And it has created the world "solitude" to express the glory of being alone.

PAUL TILLICH

Loneliness is the poverty of self; solitude is the richness of self.

MAY SARTON

Nothing will change the fact that I cannot produce the least thing without absolute solitude.

JOHANN WOLFGANG VON GOETHE

It would do the world good if every man in it would compel himself occasionally to be absolutely alone. Most of the world's progress has come out of such loneliness.

BRUCE BARTON

We need society, and we need solitude also, as we need
summer and winter, day and night, exercise and rest.

PHILIP GILBERT HAMERTON

We need quiet time to examine our lives openly and
honestly... spending quiet time alone gives your mind
an opportunity to renew itself and create order.

SUSAN L. TAYLOR

Only when one is connected to one's own core is one connected to
others. And, for me, the core, the inner spring,
can best be refound through solitude.

ANNE MORROW LINDBERGH

What a lovely surprise to finally discover
how unlonely being alone can be.

ELLEN BURSTYN

It isn't only famous movie stars who want to be alone.
Whenever I hear someone speak of privacy, I find myself thinking
once again how real and deep the need for such times is for all
human beings... at all ages.

FRED ROGERS

**The best thinking has been done in solitude.
The worst has been done in turmoil.**

THOMAS EDISON

**Conversation enriches the understanding,
but solitude is the school of genius.**

EDWARD GIBBON

**Great decisions in the realms of thought and
momentous discoveries and solutions of problems
are only possible to an individual working in solitude.**

SIGMUND FREUD

**There are voices which we hear in solitude, but they grow faint and
inaudible as we enter into the world.**

RALPH WALDO EMERSON

**A master needs quiet. Calm and quiet are his most imperative
needs. Isolation and complete loneliness are my only consolation,
and my salvation.**

RICHARD WAGNER

**If the mind loves solitude, it has thereby acquired a loftier
character, and it becomes nobler when the taste is indulged in.**

WILHELM VON HUMBOLDT

I never found the companion
that was so companionable as solitude.

HENRY DAVID THOREAU

The great man is he who, in the midst of the world,
keeps with perfect sweetness the independence of solitude.

RALPH WALDO EMERSON

Never be afraid to sit awhile and think.

LORRAINE HANSBERRY

Meditation is the soul's perspective glass.

OWEN FELLTHAM

Contemplation is the highest form of activity.

ARISTOTLE

Sit in reverie, and watch the changing color of the waves
that break upon the idle seashore of the mind.

HENRY WADSWORTH LONGFELLOW

Happiness is a butterfly which, when pursued,
is always beyond our grasp, but which, if you will
sit down quietly, may alight upon you.

NATHANIEL HAWTHORNE

You do not need to leave your room. Remain sitting
at your table and listen. Do not even listen, simply wait.
Do not even wait, be quite still and solitary. The world will
freely offer itself to you to be unmasked, it has no choice,
it will roll in ecstasy at your feet.

FRANZ KAFKA

Ah! There's nothing like staying home for real comfort.

JANE AUSTEN

I sat in my sunny doorway from sunrise till noon, rapt in a reverie
amidst the pines and hickories and sumacs, in undisturbed solitude
and stillness, while the birds sing around or flitted noiseless
through the house... I grew in those seasons like corn in the night.

HENRY DAVID THOREAU

Solitude is a silent storm that breaks down
all our dead branches; yet it sends our living roots
deeper into the living heart of the living earth.

KAHLIL GIBRAN

Solitude is the place of purification.

MARTIN BUBER

Like water which can clearly mirror the sky and the trees only
so long as its surface is undisturbed, the mind can only reflect the
true image of the Self when it is tranquil and wholly relaxed.

INDRA DEVI

In the solitude of your mind are the answers to all your questions
about life. You must take the time to ask and listen.

BAWA MUHAIYADDEEN

Unlike achieving things worth having, to achieve things
worth being usually requires long periods of solitude.

MEYER FRIEDMAN AND RAY ROSENMAN

There is one art of which man should be master,
the art of reflection.

SAMUEL TAYLOR COLERIDGE

I love people. I love my family, my children... but inside myself
is a place where I live all alone and that's where you renew
your springs that never dry up.

PEARL S. BUCK

It is in deep solitude that I find the gentleness
with which I can truly love my brothers.

THOMAS MERTON

Get away from the crowd when you can. Keep yourself to yourself,
if only for a few hours daily.

ARTHUR BRISBANE

You must have a room or a certain hour of the day or so
where you do not know what was in the morning paper...
a place where you can simply experience and bring forth
what you are, and what you might be.

JOSEPH CAMPBELL

[Going on retreat] has something to do with an aspect within each one of us... unknown to science... that longs to be at peace.

DAVID A. COOPER

In solitude we give passionate attention to our lives, to our memories, to the details around us.

VIRGINIA WOOLF

When we cannot bear to be alone, it means we do not properly value the only companion we will have from birth to death—ourselves.

EDA LESHAN

When I dance, I dance, when I sleep, I sleep; yes, and when I walk alone in a beautiful orchard, if my thoughts drift to far-off matters for some part of the time, for some other part I lead them back again to the walk, the orchard, to the sweetness of this solitude, to myself.

MICHEL DE MONTAIGNE

I will tell you what I learned myself. For me a long, five- or six-mile walk helps. And one must go alone and every day.

BRENDA UELAND

All walking is discovery.
On foot we take the time to see things whole.

HAL BORLAND

The best remedy for those who are afraid, lonely or unhappy is to go outside, somewhere where they can be quiet, alone with the heavens, nature and God. Because only then does one feel that all is as it should be and that God wishes to see people happy, amidst the simple beauty of nature.

ANNE FRANK

One can be instructed in society,
one is inspired only in solitude.

JOHANN WOLFGANG VON GOETHE

Shun Perfection

The game is supposed to be fun. If you have a bad day,
don't worry about it. You can't expect to get a hit every game.

YOGI BERRA

You're only human, you're supposed to make mistakes.

BILLY JOEL

How much of our lives is frittered away—spoiled, spent,
or sullied—by our neurotic insistence on perfection?

SARAH BAN BREATHNACH

Perfectionism is the voice of the oppressor, the enemy of the people.
It will keep you cramped and insane your whole life.

ANNE LAMOTT

Perfection does not exist.
To understand this is the triumph of human intelligence;
to expect to possess it is the most dangerous kind of madness.

ALFRED DE MUSSET

Perfection is an elusive butterfly. When we cease to demand
perfection, the business of being happy becomes that much easier.

HELEN KELLER

People throw away what they could have by
insisting on perfection, which they cannot have,
and looking for it where they will never find it

EDITH SCHAEFFER

Have no fear of perfection—you'll never reach it.

SALVADOR DALI

Striving for excellence motivates you;
striving for perfection is demoralizing.

HARRIET BERYL BRAIKER

A man would do nothing if he waited until he could do it so well
that no one could find fault.

JOHN HENRY NEWMAN

Perfection consists not in doing extraordinary things,
but in doing ordinary things extraordinarily well.

ANGELIQUE ARNAULD

Don't be afraid to admit that you are less than perfect.
It is this fragile thread that binds us to each other.

BRIAN DYSON

What, after all, is a halo? It's only one more thing to keep clean. ✓

CHRISTOPHER FRY

When everything has to be right, something isn't.

STANISLAW LEC

Life does not have to be perfect to be wonderful.

ANNETTE FUNICELLO

A good garden may have some weeds.

THOMAS FULLER

Go slowly, breathe and smile.

THICH NHAT HANH

**Life is not a race, but a journey to be
savored each step of the way.**

BRIAN DYSON

**In the name of God,
stop a moment, cease your work, look around you.**

LEO TOLSTOY

**Slow down and enjoy life. It's not only
the scenery you miss by going too fast—you also miss
the sense of where you're going and why.**

EDDIE CANTOR

**One of the benefits that comes from slowing down our lives
is that it gives us the opportunity to get back in touch with
who we really are and what we're doing here.**

ELAINE ST. JAMES

There's a lot we can do in the fast lane—we can grow
and we can expand. But we cannot deepen, and we cannot
integrate our experiences, unless we slow down.

ANGELES ARRIEN

When we get too caught up in the busyness of the world, we lose
connection with one another—and ourselves.

JACK KORNFIELD

You can come to understand your purpose in life by slowing down
and feeling your heart's desires.

MARCIA WIEDER

When we lack proper time for the simple pleasures of life,
for the enjoyment of eating, drinking, playing, creating,
visiting friends, and watching children at play,
then we have missed the purpose of life.

ED HAYES

There is more to life than increasing its speed.

MAHATMA GANDHI

As technology continues to speed up our lives, we become
more and more stressed because we are unable physically
to go as fast as our machines would allow. Yet, we try
and try to keep up, only to fall further behind.

LOIS LEVY

I think God's going to come down
and pull civilization over for speeding.

STEVEN WRIGHT

Just as your car runs more smoothly and requires less energy
to go faster and farther when the wheels are in perfect alignment,
you perform better when your thoughts, feelings,
emotions, goals, and values are in balance.

BRIAN TRACY

Live a balanced life—learn some and think some and draw and
paint and sing and dance and play and work every day some.

ROBERT FULGHUM

Balance is the perfect state of still water. Let that be our model. It
remains quiet within and is not disturbed on the surface.

CONFUCIUS

Most men pursue pleasure with such breathless haste
they hurry past it.

SØREN KIERKEGAARD

Whoever is in a hurry shows that the thing he is about
is too big for him.

PHILIP DORMER STANHOPE

Slow down and everything you are chasing
will come around and catch you.

ANONYMOUS

Have patience. Everything is difficult before it is easy.

SAADI

Be patient.
You'll know when it's time for you to wake up and move ahead.

RAM DASS

It is important from time to time to slow down,
to go away by yourself, and simply be.

EILEEN CADDY

Life is all about timing... the unreachable becomes reachable,
the unavailable become available, the unattainable... attainable.
Have the patience, wait it out. It's all about timing.

STACEY CHARTER

If they try to rush me, I always say,
"I've only got one other speed—and it's slower."

GLENN FORD

Hurrying up and using a lot of shortcuts
doesn't get us very far at all.

FRED ROGERS

Her life was like running on a treadmill or riding on
a stationary bike; it was aerobic, it was healthy,
but she wasn't going anywhere.

JULIA PHILLIPS

Have patience! In time, even grass becomes milk.

CHARAN SINGH

Learn the art of patience. Apply discipline to your thoughts
when they become anxious over the outcome of a goal. Impatience
breeds anxiety, fear, discouragement and failure. Patience creates
confidence, decisiveness and a rational outlook,
which eventually leads to success.

BRIAN ADAMS

Patience is the companion of wisdom.

SAINT AUGUSTINE

There are three secrets to managing.
The first secret is have patience. The second is be patient.
And the third most important secret is patience.

CHUCK TANNER

The key to everything is patience.
You get the chicken by hatching the egg, not by smashing it.

ARNOLD H. GLASGOW

Have patience with all things,
But, first of all with yourself.

ST. FRANCIS DE SALES

If you are patient in one moment of anger,
you will escape a hundred days of sorrow.

CHINESE PROVERB

Adopt the pace of nature; her secret is patience.

RALPH WALDO EMERSON

The trees that are slow to grow bear the best fruit.

MOLIÈRE

Nature always takes her time.
Great oaks don't become great overnight.

ANDREW MATTHEWS

With time and patience the mulberry leaf becomes a silk gown.

CHINESE PROVERB

Everything that slows us down and forces patience, everything that sets us back into the slow circles of nature, is a help.

MAY SARTON

Life is not a race, so take it slower,
hear the music before the song is over.

ANONYMOUS

Death is nature's way of telling you to slow down.

ANONYMOUS

For fast acting relief, try slowing down.

LILY TOMLIN

**There is no trouble so great or grave
that cannot be much diminished by a nice cup of tea.**

BERNARD-PAUL HEROUX

**The spirit of the tea beverage is one of peace,
comfort and refinement.**

ARTHUR GRAY

Tea was such a comfort.

EDNA ST. VINCENT MILLAY

**Tea and books—Mmmmmm, two of life's exquisite pleasures
that together bring near-bliss.**

CHRISTINE HANRAHAN

**China tea, the scent of hyacinths, wood fires and bowls
of violets—that is my mental picture of an agreeable
February afternoon.**

CONSTANCE SPRY

Thank God for tea! What would the world do without tea?
—how did it exist? I am glad I was not born before tea.

SYDNEY SMITH

Take rest; a field that has rested gives a bountiful crop.

OVID

Tea pot is on, the cups are waiting,
Favorite chairs anticipating,
No matter what I have to do,
My friend there's always time for you.

ANONYMOUS

We spend most of our time and energy in a kind of horizontal
thinking. We move along the surface of things... [but] there are
times when we stop. We sit sill. We lose ourselves in a pile of leaves
or its memory. We listen and breezes from a whole other
world begin to whisper.

JAMES CARROLL

A day out-of-doors, someone I love to talk with, a good book and some simple food and music—that would be rest.

ELEANOR ROOSEVELT

One must be out-of-doors enough to get experience of wholesome reality, as a ballast to thought and sentiment. Health requires this relaxation, this aimless life.

HENRY DAVID THOREAU

To sit in the shade on a fine day, and look upon verdure, is the most perfect refreshment.

JANE AUSTEN

All the trouble in the world is due to the fact that man cannot sit still in a room.

BLAISE PASCAL

If you get gloomy, just take an hour off and sit and think how much better this world is than hell. Of course, it won't cheer you up if you expect to go there.

DON MARQUIS

If you are losing your leisure, look out;
you may be losing your soul.

LOGAN P. SMITH

It is in his pleasure that a man really lives; it is from his leisure
that he constructs the true fabric of self.

AGNES REPPLIER

Leisure is a form of silence, not noiselessness. It is the silence
of contemplation such as occurs when we let our minds rest on
a rosebud, a child at play, a Divine mystery, or a waterfall.

BISHOP FULTON J. SHEEN

Downtime is where we become ourselves, looking into
the middle distance, kicking at the curb, lying on the grass or
sitting on the stoop and staring at the tedious blue of the summer
sky. I don't believe you can write poetry, or compose music,
or become an actor without downtime, and plenty of it, a hiatus
that passes for boredom but is really the quiet moving of the
wheels inside that fuel creativity.

ANNA QUINDLEN

People would have more leisure time if it weren't for all the
leisure-time activities that use it up.

PEG BRACKEN

To be able to fill leisure intelligently is the last product
of civilization, and at present very few people
have reached this level.

BERTRAND RUSSELL

This art of resting the mind and the power of dismissing from it
all care and worry is probably one of the secrets of energy
in our great men.

J. A. HADFIELD

A violin cannot play a sweet note unless the strings are
under pressure. But if you put too much pressure on the strings,
they snap. So do we. When the violin is not being used, you release
the tension on the strings. We, too, need periods of relaxation
to recover and renew.

TANYA WHEWAY

Tension is who you think you should be.
Relaxation is who you are.

CHINESE PROVERB

Distract your mind when you're under pressure.
Do something frivolous, nonstressful and unrelated to
"real life." Watch an old movie on TV, play with your dog,
do a crossword puzzle, take a long swim.

SHARON GOLD

How beautiful it is to do nothing, and then rest afterward.

SPANISH PROVERB

No matter how much pressure you feel at work, if you could find
ways to relax for at least five minutes every hour,
you'd be more productive.

JOYCE BROTHERS

Every now and then go away, have a little relaxation, for when you
come back to your work your judgment will be surer. Go some distance away because then the work appears smaller and more of it
can be taken in at a glance and a lack of harmony and proportion is
more readily seen.

LEONARDO DA VINCI

If a man insisted always on being serious, and never allowed
himself a bit of fun and relaxation, he would go mad
or become unstable without knowing it.

HERODOTUS

What I dream of is an art of balance, of purity and serenity
devoid of troubling or depressing subject matter—a soothing,
calming influence on the mind, rather like a good armchair
which provides relaxation from physical fatigue.

HENRI MATISSE

During [these] periods of relaxation after concentrated intellectual
activity, the intuitive mind seems to take over and can produce the
sudden clarifying insights which give so much joy and delight.

FRITJOF CAPRA

It is better to have loafed and lost
than never to have loafed at all.

JAMES THURBER

No day is so bad it can't be fixed with a nap.

CARRIE SNOW

I usually take a two hour nap from one to four.

YOGI BERRA

There is more refreshment and stimulation in a nap, even of the briefest, than in all the alcohol ever distilled.

OVID

Think what a better world it would be if we all, the whole world, had cookies and milk about three o'clock every afternoon and then lay down on our blankets for a nap.

BARBARA JORDAN

Stress is an ignorant state. It believes that everything is an emergency. Nothing is that important. Just lie down.

NATALIE GOLDBERG

Lie down and listen to the crabgrass grow,
the faucet leak, and learn to leave them so.

MARYA MANNES

It is well to lie fallow for a while.

MARTIN FARQUHAR TUPPER

Learn to pause... or nothing worthwhile will catch up to you.

DOUG KING

Learning to ignore things is one of the great paths to inner peace.

ROBERT J. SAWYER

There must be quite a few things a hot bath won't cure,
but I don't know many of them.

SYLVIA PLATH

A vacation is what you take when you can no longer
take what you've been taking.

EARL WILSON

You must have been warned against letting the golden hours slip by.
Yes, but some of them are golden only because we let them slip.

J. M. BARRIE

The time to relax is when you don't have time for it.

SYDNEY J. HARRIS

**Simplicity is making the journey of this life
with just baggage enough.**

CHARLES DUDLEY WARNER

Index

A

Adams, Brian 117
Adams, James Truslow 91
Adler, Mortimer 25
Albom, Mitch 91
Allen, Steve 61
Amen, Daniel 35
Amiel, Henri Frederic 81
Amundsen, Chris 34
Anonymous 16, 19, 44,
    56, 64, 69, 90, 115,
    119, 123
Arendt, Hannah 46
Aristotle 47, 101
Arnauld, Angelique 109
Arrien, Angeles 113
Aslett, Don 71
Asquith, Herbert Henry 56
Aurelius, Marcus 45
Austen, Jane 102, 124

B

Bagehot, Walter 91
Ban Breathnach, Sarah 66, 73,
    78, 108
Barrie, J. M. 131
Barton, Bruce 98
Baruch, Bernard 28
Beecher, Henry Ward 16, 39, 42
Befera, Lynn 33
Benavente, Jacinto 70
Bennett, Arnold 56
Berra, Yogi 44, 108, 129
Berry, John 53
Bhagavad-Gita 46
Binstead, Arthur 22
Bishop, Jim 19
Blaine, Neil 78
Bledsoe, Cedric 82
Bohn, H. G. 50
Bonaparte, Napoleon 72
Bonnano, Margaret 12
Borland, Hal 106

C

D

John-Roger 52, 67
Johnson, Samuel 25
Jordan, Barbara 129

K

Kabat-Zinn, Jon 36, 77
Kafka, Franz 102
Kalidasa 13
Keillor, Garrison 68
Keller, Helen 95, 108
Kempis, Thomas á 83
Kent, Corita 11, 17
Keyes, Jr., Ken 66
Kierkegaard, Søren 115
King, Doug 130
King, Jr., Martin Luther 89
Knebel, Fletcher 15
Knox, Frank 46
Konner, Melvin 23
Kornfield, Jack 46, 51, 113
Kübler-Ross, Elisabeth 14, 96

L

La Rochefoucauld,
    Francois, duc de 31

Lamott, Anne 108
Lao-Tzu 23, 25, 56, 65, 68, 71, 84
Larson, Doug 38
Lawrence, D. H. 94
Lawrence-Lightfoot, Sara 94
Lec, Stanislaw 110
LeGuin, Ursula 58
Lenclos, Anne de 15
LeShan, Eda 105
Levy, Lois 114
Lin Yutang 22, 25
Lin-Chi 79
Lincoln, Abraham 20
Lindbergh, Ann Morrow 83, 95, 99
Little, Mary Wilson 27
Longfellow, Henry Wadsworth 83, 102
Longworth, Alice Roosevelt 82
Lord, Shirley 30
Lowell, James Russell 52
Lowry, Mary 92
Luhrs, Janet 27
Luke 6:37 42
Lynd, Robert 60

M

Mandino, Og 26
Mannes, Marya 130

U

Ueland, Brenda 106
Undset, Sigrid 69

V

van der Rohe, Mies 28
van Dyke, Henry 40
Voltaire 11
von Humboldt, Wilhelm 100

W

Wagner, Richard 64, 100
Ward, William A. 45
Warner, Charles Dudley 38, 79, 133
Webster, Jean 38
Wheway, Tanya 126
Whitehead, Alfred North 18
Whitman, Walt 38
Wieder, Marcia 113
Wild, Ron 57
Wilde, Oscar 45, 84
Wilder, Laura Ingalls 77, 78

Wilder, Louise Beebe 23
Wilson, Earl 32, 130
Wilson, Lloyd Lee 37
Winfrey, Oprah 12, 27
Wittgenstein, Ludwig 85
Wooden, John 51
Woolf, Virginia 105
Wright, Steven 67, 114

Y

Yogananda, Paramahansa 69
Young, Margaret 30
Yunmen 81

Z

Zen Saying 90

ABOUT THE AUTHOR

Allen Klein is an award-winning professional speaker, best-selling author, and the President of the Association for Applied and Therapeutic Humor (www.aath.org). He teaches people worldwide how to use humor to deal with not-so-funny stuff. In addition to this book, Klein is also the author of *Quotations to Cheer You Up When the World is Getting You Down*, *Up Words for Down Days*, *The Change-Your-Life Quote Book*, *The Lift-Your-Spirits Quote Book*, *The Celebrate-Your-Life Quote Book*, and *Wise and Witty Words*, among others.

For more information about Klein or his presentations go to www.allenklein.com, Email him at humor@allenklein.com, or write him at 1034 Page Street, San Francisco, CA 94117.